Primarily Speaking:

Learning Activities

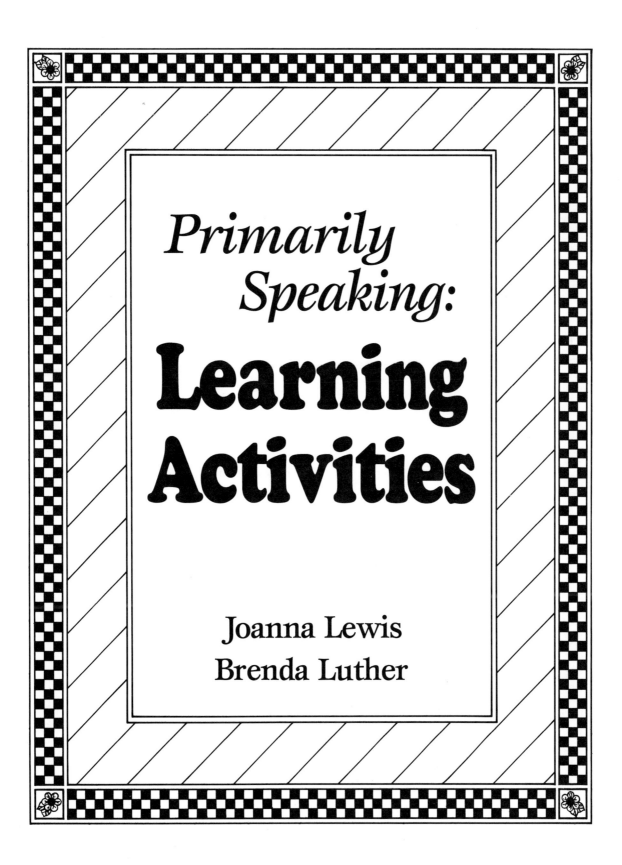

Primarily Speaking:
Learning Activities

Joanna Lewis
Brenda Luther

Bookcraft
Salt Lake City, Utah

Library of Congress Catalog Card Number: 89-83387

ISBN 0-88494-718-1

Second Printing, 1990

Printed in the United States of America

DEDICATION

They keep us busy and happy.
They give us a good reason for getting up in the
morning, and staying up all night.
Their hugs and kisses (however sloppy) give us
the energy to keep going.
They are the people who call us Mommy.
To Erin, Kristin, Dustin, Teresa, and Brandon;
to Marcey, Mitch, Karlee, Kimber, and Shandi—to these
we dedicate this book with lots of love.

REVERENCE

The first section of our book is on reverence. Many families and Primaries in the Church need a little help with reverence.

We have compiled a group of ideas specifically designed to teach children the importance of reverence. First there is a story on reverence. Next, as in the other sections, the story is written in condensed form for young storytellers. There are also some games and incentive ideas to make reverence fun and exciting to learn.

We have truly loved putting these ideas together. We hope it fills some of your reverence needs.

REVERENCE

REVERENCE

"I Can Be Reverent"
"I Can Be Reverent"

"I Can Be Reverent"

"There go those three giggly girls," someone at school was saying. "They are the best of friends, but boy are they silly!"

Paula, Kerri, and Becky were the best of friends. They had so much in common. They all lived on the same block and did everything together. They went to the same school; in fact, they were even in the same class. They liked the same music groups and would sing loud when one of their favorite songs played on the radio. Hot pink and purple were all three girls' favorite colors. They were all even in the same Valiant B class in Primary. You hardly ever saw one girl without the other two.

It was great that these girls were such good friends. Friendship is something we should all treasure. The problem with this friendship was that it was a very noisy one. Whenever or wherever the girls were, they were always talking and giggling. In the streets, in each other's homes, at school, on the bus, and even in church, these girls giggled, giggled, giggled.

Their teacher at school finally had to put their desks in three separate corners of the room to keep them quiet. Their mothers had learned to live with the giggling problem. But their poor Primary teacher, Brother Davis, was very frustrated with this constant giggling. He gave lecture after lecture about how we need to be more reverent in Primary class. He tried splitting the girls up, but they would always wind up passing notes back and forth. He tried having another adult come in and help, which did help some, but it made Brother Davis nervous.

Brother Davis was glad that the next Sunday was going to be stake conference. He would finally get a break from all the giggling.

As Brother Davis finished his Primary lesson, he said, "Remember that next week is stake conference. The men who will speak are our Heavenly Father's chosen leaders, and we should all listen and do exactly what they tell us to do. Good-bye class." With that, the class was up and out of the door.

Brother Davis called Paula back for just a minute. He looked at her for a moment, then said, "You seem to be a leader among the children in our Primary class. I think if you decided to be more reverent, the rest of the class would follow your example."

Paula shrugged her shoulders and said, "I've got to go, Brother Davis. Kerri and Becky are waiting for me."

"Okay, Paula," Brother Davis said sadly. "But remember what I told you today."

Paula did remember what Brother Davis had said to her. She thought about it all week long. In fact, she was still thinking about it when she and her family arrived at the stake center for conference. As they entered the chapel, Paula looked all over for Becky or Kerri. She couldn't see either of them, so she had to sit by her parents.

Stake conference started in the usual way. They took care of some business, and then there was a pretty musical number. The first speaker talked on how important it was to keep a personal journal. He even gave some ideas to make writing in our journals more fun. Since Paula had to keep a personal journal for her Valiant B class, she got a lot out of that talk.

The next talk was all about—wouldn't you know?—reverence. Paula thought all the speaker's remarks were pointed directly at her. He spoke of how reverence is a very special feeling that comes from deep inside us. He said, "We are not necessarily being reverent just because we are being quiet. Our minds and our hearts must be centered on heavenly things rather than worldly things." One part of his talk really touched Paula. It was when he talked about how Latter-day Saints especially should be a reverent people. He said, "We should be reverent in our homes, in our schools, in all public places, and most of all in our churches and temples. No one need think that reverence doesn't pertain to him."

Paula sat very still in her chair. She knew that what he had said was true. She also knew that Heavenly Father wanted her to change her ways. If what Brother Davis had said was true about her being a leader, she had a great responsibility ahead of her. She bowed her head right then and offered a little prayer. "Dear Heavenly Father," she began, "please forgive me for being so irreverent in the past. I want to do better. I want to be a reverent person. Please help me." Immediately she knew what she must do. She must be that example Brother Davis had talked about.

All week long she kept telling herself, "I can be reverent; I can be reverent; I can be reverent." And it worked. Her friends and teacher and mother all saw a big difference in her. Paula's mother and teacher were thrilled at the change, but Kerri and Becky were sort of shocked. But, just as Brother Davis had said, they started to follow Paula's example.

When Sunday finally came, Paula was ready to be the most reverent girl her ward had ever seen. Whenever she was tempted to talk or giggle, she'd tell herself over and over again, "I can be reverent; I can be reverent; I can be reverent." And she got much more out of the lessons and talks.

During her Primary class, not one note was passed nor one giggle giggled. Brother Davis was surprised at the change in his class. When class was over, he asked Paula to stay again. He said, "What happened this week to change you?"

"I want to be a reverent person, Brother Davis—and be the example you said I was." Paula said. "It is as simple as that."

When Paula left the room, Brother Davis looked heavenward and said, "Oh, thank you, Heavenly Father." Then, without even thinking, he let out the biggest giggle you have ever heard.

INSTRUCTIONS

Make one copy of each picture on cardstock paper. Color as desired. Laminate and cut out the pictures. Glue a large craft stick on the back of each picture.

These characters were designed especially for this story, but they can be used as visual aids for other stories.

Store the pictures in a file.

"I Can Be Reverent"
"I Can Be Reverent"
"I Can Be Reverent"

Condensed Version

"There goes those three giggly girls," said someone. Paula, Kerri, and Becky were the best of friends. They had so much in common with each other. They were always together, talking and giggling.

The adults in their lives were very frustrated by all their giggling. Brother Davis, their Primary teacher, was especially frustrated. He had tried all sorts of things to stop the girls from disrupting his class, but nothing worked.

Brother Davis was glad when next Sunday was going to be stake conference. He needed a break from all the giggling. He told the class to be sure and attend conference and listen to all the wonderful speakers.

Paula and her family did attend conference. Paula looked all around for Kerri and Becky, but she couldn't find them anywhere. Instead, she had to sit by her parents.

The speakers were very good. One man talked on reverence. He spoke of how we should be reverent wherever we are. He said that Latter-day Saints should be especially reverent. His talk really touched Paula. She knew she needed to change her ways. She knew that she, Kerri, and Becky needed to stop giggling so much and to be more reverent. She decided to try to set an example for the other girls.

All week long Paula kept telling herself, "I can be reverent; I can be reverent; I can be reverent," and it really helped. Everyone noticed a big change in her. Kerri and Becky even started to follow her example.

When Sunday finally came, Paula was ready to be the most reverent girl the ward had ever seen. Paula noticed that she got a lot more out of the talks and lessons when she was being reverent.

During Primary class the three girls were very reverent. Brother Davis couldn't believe the change. He asked Paula what had happened to change her and her friends.

Paula said, "I want to be a reverent person and to be an example to others. It's as simple as that."

When Paula left the room, Brother Davis looked heavenward and said, "Oh, thank you, Heavenly Father." Then, without even thinking, he let out the biggest giggle you have ever heard.

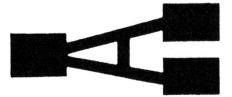

Game

Preparation: Make a copy of each page on cardstock paper. Laminate all pages. Cut each page along the dotted lines.

Game Rules: Divide the group into two teams. Also divide the cards into two piles—one pile with all the question cards, and the other pile with all the letter cards. The first team then picks a card from each pile and reads the question card. The answer to the drawn question card must begin with the letter on the letter card. When one team answers a question correctly, they keep that question card but return the letter card to the bottom of the pile. The team with the most question cards at the end of the game wins.

K O

J N

I M

H L

T

Y

S

W

R

A

P

U

Name a reverent feeling.

Name a noise that causes irreverence.

Where should we be reverent?

Where should we be quiet?

Name someone in the scriptures who was loving and thoughtful.

We must always be reverent in the temples. Name one of the temples.

Name a friend who is reverent and quiet.

Name something you should *not* take to church.

Heavenly Father made many wonderful things in nature. Name one of them.

Where can we learn about reverence?

We should never bring an animal to church. Name an animal.

Who can teach us about being quiet and peaceful?

Our prophets are good examples of reverence. Name a prophet (first, middle, or last name).

Our world is full of beautiful colors. Name a color.

General Authorities remind us to be reverent. Name a General Authority (first, middle, or last name).

Hymns can give us a feeling of reverence. Name a hymn (or a word in the title).

Families can have special experiences together. Name a place your family likes to go.

When we're reverent, we can think about our blessings. Name one of your blessings.

Respect is a part of reverence and care. Name someone or something you respect.

We can be reverent at home. Name a way to be reverent at home.

We should be reverent when we pray. When or where can we pray?

Primary songs can give us a feeling of reverence. Name a Primary song (or a word in the title).

Reverence can make us feel grateful. Name someone or something you are grateful for.

We can show our Heavenly Father how much we love him by being reverent. Name another person you love.

Reverent Children

Make a copy of both reverent children on cardstock paper. Color and laminate them. These were designed to be used for any of your reverence needs.

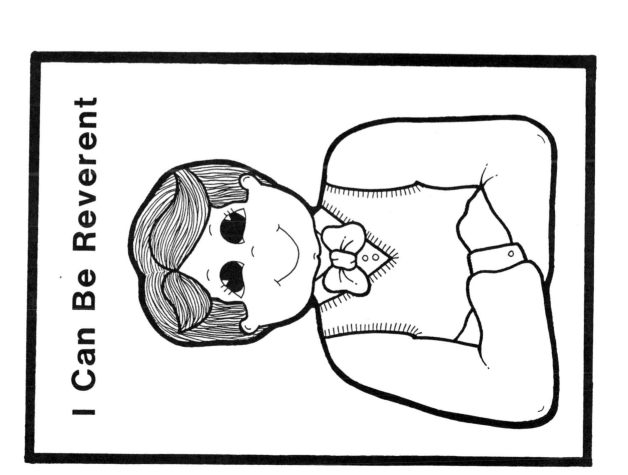

I Can Be Reverent

I Can Be Reverent

Labels

Can Labels: The "Reverence Can" labels were designed to fit on small soup cans. Make a copy of each on a desired color of paper. Wrap it around a can and securely glue it on. Use it as an incentive, a reward can, or just a cute centerpiece.

REVERENCE

Ingredients:

Quiet, peaceful thoughts, respect, gratitude, patience, prayerful study, happiness and blessings too numerous to list.

Valiants 'Can' Be Reverent

Great Value

Net Wt. 12 Oz.

No Expiration Date

Nutrition Information:

Vitamin Q	100%
Vitamin U	100%
Vitamin I	100%
Vitamin E	100%
Vitamin T	100%
Low in Noise	

REVERENCE

Nutrition Information:

Vitamin Q	100%
Vitamin U	100%
Vitamin I	100%
Vitamin E	100%
Vitamin T	100%
Low in Noise	

No Expiration Date

CTR's "Can Be Reverent"

Great Value

Net Wt. 12 Oz.

Ingredients:

Quiet, peaceful thoughts, respect, gratitude, patience, prayerful study, happiness and blessings too numerous to list.

REVERENCE

Ingredients:
Quiet, peaceful thoughts, respect, gratitude, patience, prayerful study, happiness and blessings too numerous to list.

Merrie Misses 'Can' Be Reverent

Nutrition Information:

Vitamin Q	100%
Vitamin U	100%
Vitamin I	100%
Vitamin E	100%
Vitamin T	100%
Low in Noise	

Great Value

Net Wt. 12 Oz.

No Expiration Date

REVERENCE

Nutrition Information:

Vitamin Q	100%
Vitamin U	100%
Vitamin I	100%
Vitamin E	100%
Vitamin T	100%
Low in Noise	

Blazers 'Can' Be Reverent

Great Value

No Expiration Date

Net Wt. 12 Oz.

Ingredients:
Quiet, peaceful thoughts, respect, gratitude, patience, prayerful study, happiness and blessings too numerous to list.

REVERENCE

Right Label

Ingredients:
Quiet, peaceful thoughts, respect, gratitude, patience, prayerful study, happiness and blessings too numerous to list.

|||| 1 2 3 4 5

REVERENCE

I 'Can' Be Reverent

Net Wt. 12 Oz.

Great Value

Nutrition Information:

Vitamin Q	100%
Vitamin U	100%
Vitamin I	100%
Vitamin E	100%
Vitamin T	100%
Low in Noise	

No Expiration Date

Left Label

Nutrition Information:

Vitamin Q	100%
Vitamin U	100%
Vitamin I	100%
Vitamin E	100%
Vitamin T	100%
Low in Noise	

No Expiration Date

REVERENCE

Families 'Can' Be Reverent

Great Value

Net Wt. 12 Oz.

Ingredients:
Quiet, peaceful thoughts, respect, gratitude, patience, prayerful study, happiness and blessings too numerous to list.

|||| 1 2 3 4 5

Large Can Label: Make a copy of the large can label in any desired color. Cover a large can or canister with construction paper or contact paper. Glue the large label on the front.

Badges

Copy on cardstock. Laminate and cut out.

Badges

Copy on cardstock. Laminate and cut out. Add a small bow to the bottom to make it cute.

FEELINGS OF REVERENCE

3 across: REVERENCE

Across

1. What is it called when we are sitting very still and thinking about the Savior?

2. A very glad feeling inside.

3. REVERENCE

4. A calm feeling inside.

5. Singing reverent _____ gets us ready to be reverent in church.

6. Being grateful for all our blessings is showing _____ .

Down

1. Where we can go to read about reverent people who lived a long time ago.

2. When we ask and thank our Heavenly Father for things, we are being _____ .

3. Thoughtful, prayerful, and gratitude are some of the _____ of reverence.

4. How does it sound when it is reverent?

5. Great admiration for someone or something.

6. We show our _____ for our Heavenly Father when we are reverent.

The second section of our book is on the Articles of Faith.

The children in the Church need to be taught the Articles of Faith; in fact, learning them is a requirement for receiving the Gospel in Action award.

We have included a story and a poem on the Articles of Faith. Incentive charts will make learning more fun. There are also games, a certificate, and a cute little "lucky thirteen."

Take these ideas and add them to your own, and then have fun teaching your kids the Articles of Faith.

13.

We believe in being honest, true, chaste, benevolent, virtuous, and in doing good to all men; indeed, we may say that we follow the admonition of Paul ~ We believe all things, we hope all things, we have endured many things, and hope to be able to endure all things. If there is anything virtuous, lovely, or of good report or praiseworthy, we seek after these things.

Billy Believes...

"I like being a Latter-day Saint," said Billy as he bounded in from school one day. Mother smiled warmly and said, "I'm glad, Billy, so do I." Before she could say another word, Billy had grabbed three cookies and gone out of the door to play baseball with some neighborhood boys.

Billy was a little seven-year-old boy with reddish brown hair and lots of freckles on his cheeks, and he *did* like being a Latter-day Saint. He liked everything about it. He liked family home evenings and family scripture study. He liked watching his mom and dad getting ready to go to the temple, and he knew he would go there too someday. He liked going to church and watching the older boys pass the sacrament, and he especially liked fast and testimony meetings. He would often get up and bear his own testimony. But his very most favorite part of being a Latter-day Saint was being able to go to Primary. Singing the Primary songs and listening to Sister Fredrick's lessons always gave him a warm feeling inside.

One fast Sunday, Billy got up to bear his testimony. He told the members of his ward that he knew the Church was true. He said, "I believe every single thing about the Church, and I'm proud to be a Latter-day Saint." Billy had a good feeling inside as he sat back down by his parents. Billy's mother put her arm around him and gave him a tight squeeze. Billy knew she was very proud of him.

When church was over, Billy went outside to wait for his mom and dad. He liked to walk on the very edge of the sidewalk and pretend it was a tightrope. Billy's friend Jacob was outside too. He walked right up to Billy and said, "Boy, you sure are brave to get up and bear your testimony each fast Sunday."

"I sort of like to," Billy commented. He was still concentrating on the sidewalk. He didn't want to fall off before he got to the end.

"It would scare me to death," said Jacob. "How do you do it?"

"Well," said Billy, "it really isn't scary if you believe the Church is true. All you have to do is say what is in your heart."

"But how do you know the Church is true?" Jacob asked. "How can you be so sure that everything about the Church is true? We are the same age, and I am not even certain I know exactly what the Church believes in."

"Jacob, it's time to go," his mother called.

"See you later," Jacob said as he waved good-bye.

This sort of confused Billy. As he thought about it, he really wasn't sure that he knew everything that the Church believed in.

Billy was really quiet at home. When his mother asked him what was troubling him, he said, "Mom, what exactly do Latter-day Saints believe in? I know we believe in temple work, the Word of Wisdom, prophets, and the Book of Mormon, but isn't there a lot more?"

Billy's mother went to her room and came back with her copy of the Pearl of Great Price. She said, "Yes, Billy, Latter-day Saints believe in a lot more than those things you just mentioned." She went on to explain that when the Church was first organized a long time ago, the early missionaries and the Prophet Joseph Smith were often asked to explain just what the Church believed. Each one of these men would give a slightly different answer, even though they all believed the same things. They were just saying it in their own words. Sometimes this confused people. Sometimes, too, the things the missionaries would say might just be their own interpretations of the actual doctrines of the Church. "Then, in 1842, a newspaper man asked the Prophet Joseph Smith to write down what the basic beliefs of the Church were," said Mother. "The Prophet, with the Lord's help, wrote what is now known as the Articles of Faith. These thirteen articles tell us what some of our most basic beliefs are. They were first published in a newspaper, and this helped everyone understand better what the Church believed in. The Articles of Faith are now found near the end of the Pearl of Great Price."

She opened her scriptures, and she and Billy read all thirteen articles together. Billy's heart started to beat hard, and he got the warmest feeling he had ever had come over him. His eyes even started to water.

"Oh, Mom, thank you," he said. "Now I know exactly what I believe in. I can't wait to tell Jacob."

INSTRUCTIONS

Make one copy of each picture on cardstock paper. Color each as desired. Laminate and cut out the pictures. Glue a large craft stick on the back of each picture.

These characters were designed especially for this story, but they can be used as visual aids for other stories.

Store the pictures in a file.

Billy Believes...

Condensed Version

Billy is a seven-year-old boy with reddish brown hair on his head and freckles on his cheeks. He is a very good little boy, and really enjoys being a Latter-day Saint. He likes everything about it. He especially likes to bear his testimony.

One fast Sunday Billy got up and bore his testimony. He said, "I believe every single thing about the Church, and I'm proud to be a Latter-day Saint."

Billy's mother was very proud of him. She gave him a little squeeze as he sat back down.

After church, Billy's friend Jacob met him outside. "Boy, are you brave to bear your testimony every fast Sunday!" said Jacob. "I could never do it."

"I sort of like to," said Billy. "All you have to do is say what is in your heart."

"But," said Jacob, "we are the same age and I'm not even sure I know exactly what the Church believes in."

Jacob and Billy had to go home.

Billy thought a lot about what Jacob had said. Later on Billy asked his mother to explain how he could know exactly what Latter-day Saints believe in. She went to her room and came back with a copy of the Pearl of Great Price. "In the very back of this book," Mother said, "are written the thirteen Articles of Faith. They tell us what Latter-day Saints believe in."

Billy and his mother read all thirteen Articles of Faith. Billy's heart started to beat real hard, and a very warm feeling came over him. His eyes even started to water.

"Oh, thank you, Mom," said Billy. "I can't wait to tell Jacob."

THE ARTICLES OF FAITH

OF THE CHURCH OF JESUS CHRIST OF LATTER-DAY SAINTS

History of the Church, Vol. 4, pp. 535–541

WE ᵃbelieve in ᵇGod, the ᶜEternal Father, and in His ᵈSon, Jesus Christ, and in the ᵈHoly Ghost.

2 We believe that men will be ᵃpunished for their ᵇown sins, and not for Adam's ᶜtransgression.

3 We believe that through the ᵃAtonement of Christ, all ᵇmankind may be ᶜsaved, by obedience to the laws and ordinances of the Gospel.

4 We believe that the first principles and ᵃordinances of the Gospel are: first, ᵇFaith in the Lord Jesus Christ; second, ᶜRepentance; third, ᵈBaptism by ᵉimmersion for the ᶠremission of sins; fourth, Laying on of ᵍhands for the ᵇgift of the Holy Ghost.

5 We believe that a man must be ᵃcalled of God, by ᵇprophecy, and by the laying on of ᶜhands by those who are in ᵈauthority, to ᵉpreach the Gospel and administer in the ᶠordinances thereof.

6 We believe in the same ᵃorganization that existed in the Primitive Church, namely, ᵇapostles, ᶜprophets, ᵈpastors, ᵈteachers, ᵉevangelists, and so forth.

7 We believe in the ᵃgift of ᵇtongues, ᶜprophecy, ᵈrevelation, ᵉvisions, ᶠhealing, ᵍinterpretation of tongues, and so forth.

8 We believe the ᵃBible to be the ᵇword of God as far as it is translated ᶜcorrectly; we also believe the ᵈBook of Mormon to be the word of God.

9 We believe all that God has revealed, all that He does now reveal, and we believe that He will ᵃever ᵇreveal many great and important things pertaining to the Kingdom of God.

1a ᴛɢ Believe.
b ᴛɢ God the Father—Elohim; Godhead.
c ᴛɢ Jesus Christ, Divine Sonship.
d ᴛɢ Holy Ghost.
2a ᴛɢ Punishment.
b Ex. 32: 33; Deut. 24: 16; Ezek. 18: 20 (1–20). ᴛɢ Accountability; Agency.
c ᴛɢ Fall of Man.
3a ᴛɢ Jesus Christ, Atonement through.
b Jude 1: 3.
c Ps. 49: 15; Mosiah 27: 24 (24–26); D&C 93: 38; Moses 5: 9. ᴛɢ Salvation.
4a ᴛɢ Ordinances.
b D&C 138: 33. ᴛɢ Baptism, Qualifications for; Faith.
c ᴛɢ Repentance.
d ᴛɢ Baptism.

e ᴛɢ Baptism, Immersion.
f ᴛɢ Remission of Sins.
g ᴛɢ Hands, Laying on of.
h ᴛɢ Holy Ghost, Gift of.
5a Num. 27: 16 (15–20). ᴛɢ Called of God; Priesthood, Qualifying for.
b ᴛɢ Prophecy.
c ᴛɢ Hands, Laying on of.
d ᴛɢ Authority; Priesthood, Authority.
e D&C 11: 15 (15–21). ᴛɢ Preaching.
f Alma 13: 16 (8–16).
6a ᴛɢ Church Organization.
b ᴛɢ Prophets, Mission of.
c ᴛɢ Bishop.
d ᴛɢ Teachers.

e ᴛɢ Patriarchs.
7a ᴛɢ Holy Ghost, Gifts of.
b ᴛɢ Language.
c ᴛɢ Prophecy.
d ᴛɢ Revelation.
e ᴛɢ Visions.
f ᴛɢ Healing.
g 1 Cor. 12: 10; Morm... 7.
8a ᴛɢ Bible; Revelation; Scriptures, Preservation of; Scriptures, Writing of.
b Isa. 8: 20 (16–22).
c 1 Ne. 13: 26 (20–40); 14: 21 (20–26).
d ᴛɢ Book of Mormon.
9a ᴛɢ Revelation.
b Dan. 2: 28 (22–29, 40); Amos 3: 7; D&C 121: 26 (26–33). ᴛɢ Scriptures to Come Forth.

61

10 We believe in the literal ᵃgathering of Israel and in the restoration of the ᵇTen Tribes; that ᶜZion (the New Jerusalem) will be built upon the American continent; that Christ will ᵈreign personally upon the earth; and, that the earth will be ᵉrenewed and receive its ᶠparadisiacal ᵍglory.

11 We claim the ᵃprivilege of worshiping Almighty God according to the ᵇdictates of our own ᶜconscience, and allow all men the same privilege, let them ᵈworship how, where, or what they may.

12 We believe in being ᵃsubject to ᵇkings, presidents, rulers, and magistrates, in ᶜobeying, honoring, and sustaining the ᵈlaw.

13 ᵃWe believe in being ᵇhonest, true, ᶜchaste, ᵈbenevolent, virtuous, and in doing ᵉgood to all men; indeed, we may say that we follow the ᶠadmonition of Paul—We believe all things, we ᵍhope all things, we have endured many things, and hope to be able to ᵇendure all things. If there is anything ᶦvirtuous, ᵈlovely, or of good report or praiseworthy, we seek after these things.

JOSEPH SMITH.

10a Isa. 49: 22 (20–22); 60: 4; 1 Ne. 19: 16 (16–17). ᴛɢ Israel, Gathering of.
b ᴛɢ Israel, Tribes of, Ten Lost.
c Ether 13: 6 (2–11); D&C 42: 9; 45: 66 (66–67); 84: 2 (2–5); Moses 7: 62. ᴛɢ Jerusalem, New; Zion.
d Micah 4: 7. ᴛɢ Jesus Christ, Millennial Reign.
e ᴛɢ Earth, Cleansing of; Earth, Renewal of;

Eden.
f ɪᴇ a condition like the Garden of Eden; see Isa. 11: 1–9; 35: 1–10; 51: 1–3; 65: 17–25; Ezek. 36: 35 (1–38); 2 Ne. 8: 1–3. ᴛɢ Paradise.
g ᴛɢ Glory.
11a Alma 21: 22 (21–22); D&C 93: 19; 134: 4 (1–4).
b ᴛɢ Agency.
c ᴛɢ Conscience.
d Micah 4: 5; D&C 134: 7 (4, 7). ᴛɢ Worship.

12a D&C 134: 1 (1–11). ᴛɢ Citizenship; Governments.
b ᴛɢ Kings, Earthly.
c ᴛɢ Obedience.
d D&C 58: 21 (21–23).
13a Philip. 4: 8.
b ᴛɢ Honesty; Integrity.
c ᴛɢ Chastity.
d ᴛɢ Benevolence.
e ᴛɢ Good Works.
f ᴛɢ Hope.
g ᴛɢ Perseverance; Steadfastness.
h ᴛɢ Modesty; Virtue.
i ᴛɢ Beauty.

'WE BELIEVE' 'WE DO'
Game

Preparation: Make a copy of all three pages on cardstock paper. The spinner can be of any color. The other two pages must be two different colors. Laminate and cut them out. Put the spinner together with a brad-type fastener. Cut the cards along the dotted lines.

Game Rules: This game can be played in teams or as individuals. The first player spins the spinner. The number indicates which Article of Faith the "We Believe" question will be on. The player then draws a "We Believe" card and tries to answer it. If he can answer it correctly, he gets 10 points; if he cannot, he must draw a "We Do" card. He then has to try to do whatever is written on the card. If he does the "We Do," he gets 5 points; if he cannot, the other players get 5 points. Continue playing until all the Articles of Faith have been reviewed.

An extra page of cards has been included so you can make up some more "We Do" cards.

'WE BELIEVE'

Recite the whole article of faith.

'WE BELIEVE'

What is the key word to this article of faith?

'WE BELIEVE'

Recite any article of faith.

'WE BELIEVE'

Ask someone else to recite the article of faith for you (you still get the points).

'WE BELIEVE'

Read the article of faith from the scriptures.

'WE BELIEVE'

What is the last word of this article of faith?

'WE BELIEVE'

Recite this article of faith while holding your tongue.

'WE BELIEVE'

What gospel principle is this article of faith about?

'WE DO'

Rub your head and pat your tummy until your next turn.

'WE DO'

Recite the Pledge of Allegiance.

'WE DO'

Write "I love you" ten times.

'WE DO'

Say your favorite tongue twister three times.

'WE DO'

Pull a funny face.

'WE DO'

Walk across the room with a book on your head.

'WE DO'

FREE CARD
(You still get the points.)

'WE DO'

Sing one verse of "I Am a Child of God."

'WE DO'

'WE DO'

'WE DO'

'WE DO'

'WE DO'

'WE DO'

'WE DO'

'WE DO'

Lucky Thirteen

The One, the Eight, and the Ten
    were in the hall a-talking.
When around the corner came Thirteen,
    right up to them a-walking.

The numbers stood there boasting,
    about which one of them was best.
Each thought himself important,
    much better than the rest.

The One said, "I'm superior,
    more important than either of you.
There's only one true God you know,
    and that you know is true."

The Eight said, "But you're wrong dear One,
    the Eight stands above all.
Children are baptized when they are eight,
    even though they're still quite small.

The Ten proudly puffed out his chest.
    He said with much conceit,
"I represent the Ten Commandments,
    and the Ten Tribes that we seek."

The numbers all looked at poor Thirteen,
    in time to see a teardrop fall.
"I'm not a very important number.
    There's nothing special about me at all.

"Most folks think I'm unlucky.
    I'm only used to scare.
You all represent such special things,
    but I have nothing to share."

The numbers were surprised at this.
    They couldn't believe their ears.
"Why we have looked up to you, Thirteen,
    for years and years and years."

"There are thirteen original colonies," said One.
    "And thirteen stripes on old Red, White, and Blue.
President Benson is our thirteenth prophet,
    and everything he says is true."

Then the Ten spoke up both loud and clear.
    He said with wisdom in his voice,
"The most important thirteen ever written,
    were the Articles of Faith of course."

Then Thirteen wiped away his tears,
    and a smile spread across his face.
"I guess I'm lucky after all,
    I'm important to the human race."

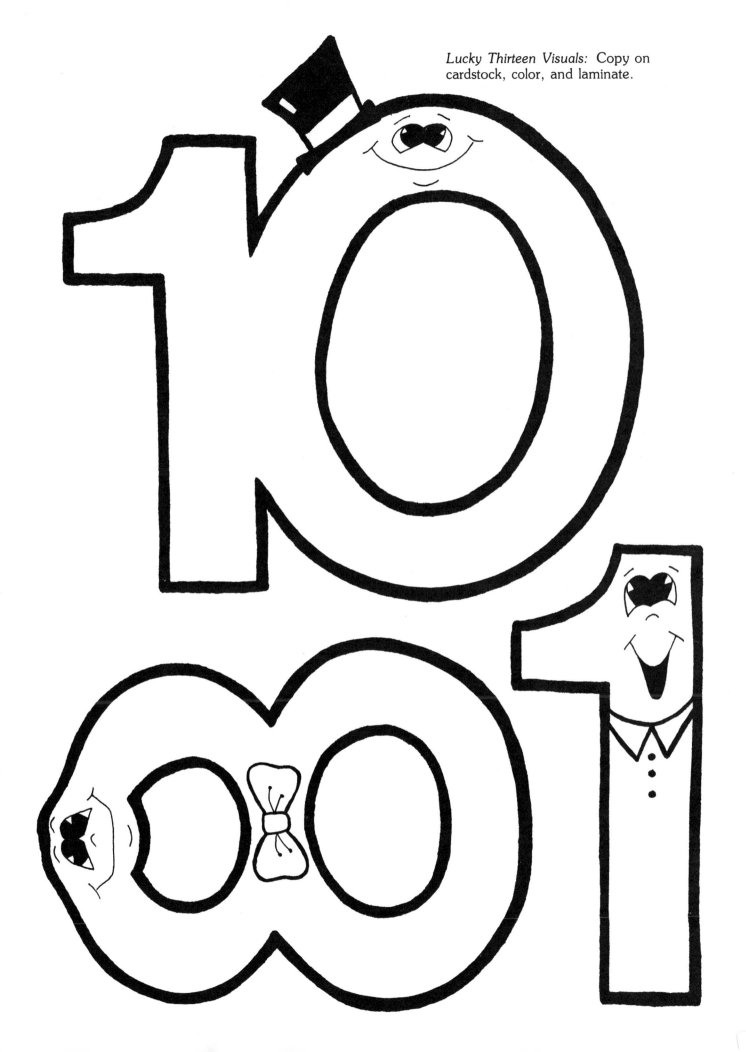

Lucky Thirteen Visuals: Copy on cardstock, color, and laminate.

Articles of Faith

We have included two sizes of the Article of Faith cards for a variety of uses. Copy them on cardstock and laminate them. Cut the small cards along the dark lines. Use the large cards as is. The key words can be used as needed.

1.

We believe in God, the Eternal Father, and in His Son, Jesus Christ, and in the Holy Ghost.

4.

We believe that the first principles and ordinances of the Gospel are: first, Faith in the Lord Jesus Christ; second, Repentance; third, Baptism by immersion for the remission of sins; fourth, laying on of hands for the gift of the Holy Ghost.

2.

We believe that men will be punished for their own sins, and not for Adam's transgression.

5.

We believe that a man must be called of God, by prophecy, and by the laying on of hands by those who are in authority, to preach the Gospel and administer in the ordinances thereof.

3.

We believe that through the Atonement of Christ, all mankind may be saved, by obedience to the laws and ordinances of the Gospel.

6.

We believe in the same organization that existed in the Primitive Church, namely, apostles, prophets, pastors, teachers, evangelists, and so forth.

7.

We believe in the gift of tongues, prophecy, revelation, visions, healing, interpretation of tongues, and so forth.

8.

We believe the Bible to be the word of God as far as it is translated correctly; we also believe the Book of Mormon to be the word of God.

9.

We believe all that God has revealed, all that He does now reveal, and we believe that He will yet reveal many great and important things pertaining to the Kingdom of God.

10.

We believe in the literal gathering of Israel and in the restoration of the Ten Tribes; that Zion (the New Jerusalem) will be built upon the American continent; that Christ will reign personally upon the earth; and, that the earth will be renewed and receive its paradisiacal glory.

11.

We claim the privilege of worshiping Almighty God according to the dictates of our own conscience, and allow all men the same privilege, let them worship how, where, or what they may.

12.

We believe in being subject to kings, presidents, rulers, and magistrates, in obeying, honoring, and sustaining the law.

13.

We believe in being honest, true, chaste, benevolent, virtuous, and in doing good to all men; indeed, we may say that we follow the admonition of Paul ~ We believe all things, we hope all things, we have endured many things, and hope to be able to endure all things. If there is anything virtuous, lovely, or of good report or praiseworthy, we seek after these things.

KEYWORDS

1. Godhead

2. Men

3. Atonement

4. First Principles

5. Hands

6. Organization

7. Gifts

8. Translate

9. Revelation

10. Ten Tribes

11. We Claim

12. Law

13. Admonition

1.

We believe in God, the Eternal Father, and in His Son, Jesus Christ, and in the Holy Ghost.

2.

We believe that men will be punished for their own sins, and not for Adam's transgression.

3.

We believe that through the Atonement of Christ, all mankind may be saved, by obedience to the laws and ordinances of the Gospel.

4.

We believe that the first principles and ordinances of the Gospel are: first, Faith in the Lord Jesus Christ; second, Repentance; third, Baptism by immersion for the remission of sins; fourth, laying on of hands for the gift of the Holy Ghost.

5.

We believe that a man must be called of God, by prophecy, and by the laying on of hands by those who are in authority, to preach the Gospel and administer in the ordinances thereof.

6.

We believe in the same organization that existed in the Primitive Church, namely, apostles, prophets, pastors, teachers, evangelists, and so forth.

2

We believe in the gift of tongues, prophecy, revelation, visions, healing, interpretation of tongues, and so forth.

8.

We believe the the Bible to be the word of God as far as it is translated correctly; we also believe the Book of Mormon to be the word of God.

9.

We believe all that God has revealed, all that He does now reveal, and we believe that He will yet reveal many great and important things pertaining to the Kingdom of God.

10.

We believe in the literal gathering of Israel and in the restoration of the Ten Tribes; that Zion (the New Jerusalem) will be built upon the American continent; that Christ will reign personally upon the earth; and, that the earth will be renewed and receive its paradisiacal glory.

11.

We claim the privilege of worshiping Almighty God according to the dictates of our own conscience, and allow all men the same privilege, let them worship how, where, or what they may.

12.

We believe in being subject to kings, presidents, rulers, and magistrates, in obeying, honoring, and sustaining the law.

13.

We believe in being honest, true, chaste, benevolent, virtuous, and in doing good to all men; indeed, we may say that we follow the admonition of Paul ~ We believe all things, we hope all things, we have endured many things, and hope to be able to endure all things. If there is anything virtuous, lovely, or of good report or praiseworthy, we seek after these things.

INCENTIVES

Make a copy for each person. Cut out all the parts. As the children learn an article of faith, let them add a bow to the kite, a scoop to the ice-cream cone, or a part to the caterpillar. The children will be able to see how much they know.

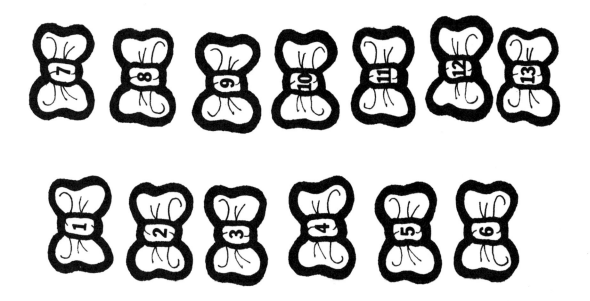

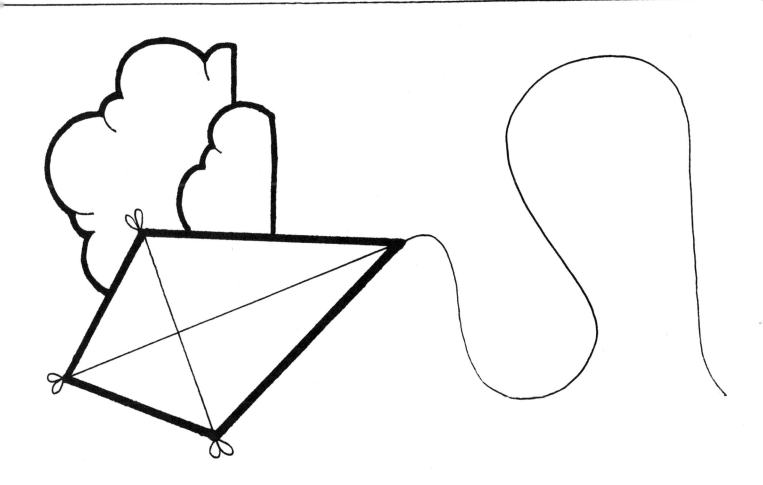

Badges

These Article of Faith badges are numbered 1 through 13 so they can be used as an incentive. As the children learn an article of faith, use a paper punch and punch out the number.

Copy on cardstock. Laminate and cut out.

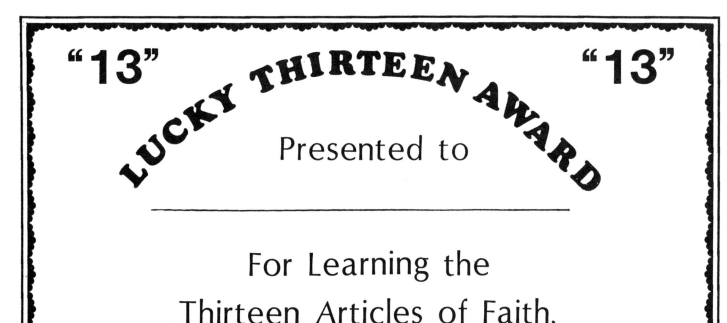

"13" "13"

LUCKY THIRTEEN AWARD

Presented to

_____

For Learning the
Thirteen Articles of Faith.

Signed _____   Date _____

Certificate

Copy on colored paper. Give to
the children whenever needed.

Refrigerator Magnet

Copy on cardstock paper.
Laminate and cut it out. Hot
glue a magnet on the back. It
makes a cute handout.

Thirteen is a

5 12 6 2 13 10 5 4 8

11 8 7 7 2 11 9

3 1 10 13 1 6

4 9 3 12

lucky number !

KEY WORD HIDE-A-WAY

A	D	M	O	N	I	T	I	O	N	A	D	W	G	J	K	T
B	R	D	A	B	H	M	O	P	G	K	C	E	C	L	K	E
H	I	T	A	T	O	N	E	M	E	N	T	F	C	D	A	N
L	H	J	I	C	L	S	X	R	S	S	A	C	B	Z	S	Q
Q	N	O	W	C	M	F	W	M	A	H	L	L	X	U	V	T
S	V	R	X	F	L	T	X	C	E	A	B	A	N	Q	P	R
G	Z	G	R	I	A	E	D	B	I	M	O	I	W	K	N	I
I	Y	A	J	C	I	J	S	Q	K	C	N	M	N	H	K	B
F	V	N	F	M	D	C	S	S	G	O	D	H	E	A	D	E
T	O	I	K	E	J	C	D	I	O	Z	N	K	B	N	A	S
S	R	Z	P	N	K	I	J	V	Y	F	K	A	C	D	C	F
P	S	A	Z	Z	V	N	J	K	I	K	S	B	A	S	J	I
Y	Q	T	R	A	N	S	L	A	T	E	V	F	X	T	Y	J
X	Y	I	Z	X	M	I	J	N	T	W	W	F	A	J	F	N
R	W	O	M	I	O	M	R	E	V	E	L	A	T	I	O	N
M	J	N	W	T	O	I	Y	X	O	F	M	O	U	B	T	U
F	I	R	S	T	O	P	R	I	N	C	I	P	L	E	S	H

Find the 13 key words hidden in the puzzle above.

Godhead	**Organization**	**Ten Tribes**
Men	**Gifts**	**We Claim**
Atonement	**Translate**	**Law**
First Principles	**Revelation**	**Admonition**
Hands		

SCRIPTURE STUDY

The last section of our book is on scripture study. Many of us struggle with this, not only with our personal scripture study but also with our family scripture study.

The scripture study section of our book contains two stories, a game, and several cute ideas on how to become a bookworm. There are bookmarks, handout ideas, and a certificate to be used as needed.

Get excited about scripture study, and those you teach will too.

The
Book
of
Mormon

SCRIPTURE STUDY

SCRIPTURE STUDY

Alarm Clocks and Chocolate Milk

Tim was ten years old and just starting the Blazer A class in Primary. He was the oldest in his family. He had two younger brothers whom he always tried to set a good example for. Tim enjoyed Scouting and being involved in all Church activities. His favorite subject in school was math, and his favorite snack was a big glass of chocolate milk. Every day after school Tim got himself a big, cool glass of chocolate milk before he did anything else.

On the third Sunday of the new year in Primary, the lesson focused on reading the scriptures. Brother Jones, Tim's Primary teacher, challenged the class to read the whole Book of Mormon that year.

"It seems as if in every *Ensign*," Brother Jones said, "in every conference and general meeting, President Benson tells us to read the Book of Mormon. You boys who accept this challenge and read the whole Book of Mormon will be ready to graduate from Primary and receive the priesthood next year."

Tim was touched by what Brother Jones had said. "Wow," thought Tim. "Next year I am going to receive the priesthood. I need to be prepared."

Tim raised his hand, along with the other boys, as they all accepted the challenge.

Tim asked his mother and father to help him fulfill this challenge. His parents were very proud of Tim for trying to read the Book of Mormon at such a young age. They agreed to help all they could.

Tim's mother set her alarm clock a half hour earlier so she could get Tim up. Tim's father was always ready and willing to answer any of Tim's questions. So the scripture study began.

Every morning Tim's mother woke him up before any of the other boys. Tim sleepily crawled out of bed, stumbled to the refrigerator, and got himself a glass of chocolate milk. This helped Tim wake up a little and be ready to read. Next he went back to his room, switched on the light, and picked up his Book of Mormon to read.

The first few days were fun and exciting. It made Tim feel good to know he was doing what the prophet wanted him to do. As the days passed, Tim started having a little trouble staying interested and understanding what all the words meant. But Tim's mother and father were always willing to help.

One Sunday, Brother Jones asked the boys how they were doing on their scripture study. Some of the boys had already given up, but not Tim. He was proud to say that he was already to 2 Nephi.

"Well," said Brother Jones. "How are you liking the scriptures?"

"Great," said Tim happily. "But sometimes I don't understand everything I'm reading."

"Are you asking for help before you start to read?" asked Brother Jones.

"Oh yes," Tim explained. "My mother and father are helping me every step of the way."

"Parents are great helpers," said Brother Jones. "But there is someone else who would love to help you. All you have to do is ask him."

"Is it Heavenly Father?" asked Tim.

"That's right," answered Brother Jones. "Every morning before you start reading, take a few minutes and kneel down and ask for his help. It works wonderfully well."

Tim tried it and it did work wonderfully well. He always had such a good feeling inside. He still did not always understand every word, but he could feel the spirit of the scriptures.

As the weeks and months passed, it became a habit for Tim to read every day. His little brothers even read their scriptures from time to time. In November of that year Tim read the last page of the Book of Mormon. That afternoon Tim called Brother Jones on the telephone and told him the good news. Brother Jones was delighted. He said, "I will be right over."

A few minutes later Brother Jones knocked at the door. He had something tucked under his arm.

"This is for you," Brother Jones said with a smile. "Go ahead and open it."

"First come and celebrate with me," Tim said. "My mom made my favorite cookies. And we can have a glass of chocolate milk."

As they shared the treat, Tim opened the package. It was a brand new copy of the Doctrine and Covenants. "Now you can keep right on with your reading," Brother Jones said.

They both laughed and drank their chocolate milk.

INSTRUCTIONS

These visual aids were designed to be used a specific way.

Copy the pictures on cardstock. Color, laminate, and cut them out along the dark lines. Hot glue a large craft stick to the back of each of the characters' heads (the scriptures and glass do not need a stick).

As you tell the story about Tim reading his scriptures, tape the scripture picture to the bottom half of the craft stick. Position the scriptures so it looks like Tim is holding and reading the book.

As you tell about Tim having a glass of chocolate milk, tape the glass to the bottom half of the craft stick. Position it so it looks like Tim is holding and drinking the milk.

Alarm Clocks and Chocolate Milk

Condensed Version

Tim was ten years old and just starting the Blazer A class in Primary. On the third Sunday of the new year, Brother Jones, Tim's Primary teacher, was giving a lesson on scripture study. He told the boys how important it was for them to read their scriptures every day. He even challenged the boys to read the whole book of Mormon that year. He said, "You boys are going to graduate from Primary next year, and then you'll receive the priesthood. You need to be prepared."

All the boys, including Tim, accepted this challenge. Tim's mother and father agreed to help him all they could. Tim's mother set her alarm clock ahead a half hour earlier so she could get Tim up to read. Tim's father was always ready and willing to answer any questions. They were very proud of Tim.

Every morning, Tim's mother woke him up early. He crawled out of bed, stumbled to the refrigerator, and got himself a glass of chocolate milk. The chocolate milk helped Tim wake up so he could start reading.

Tim read his scriptures faithfully every day. He kept going even when some of the other boys had given up. Tim realized that when he asked Heavenly Father to help him understand the scriptures, he got much more out of his reading. So Tim added prayer to his morning routine.

One day in November Tim finished the Book of Mormon. He was very excited. Tim called Brother Jones on the telephone to tell him the good news. Brother Jones was thrilled. He said he would be right over for a visit.

Brother Jones arrived with a small package for Tim. Tim said, "Come in and share a treat with me. Mom made my favorite cookies, and we can have a glass of chocolate milk."

Tim opened the package as they ate the cookies. It was a brand new copy of the Doctrine and Covenants.

"Now you can keep right on reading the scriptures," said Brother Jones.

They both laughed and drank their chocolate milk.

BOOKWORMS

A long time ago, there lived a little worm. Like many worms, he liked to eat apples. There was one thing he liked to eat even more than apples, and that was books.

In the home where he lived, there were lots of books sitting around. Books sat on tables, in drawers, on shelves, and in boxes. These were the kind of books the little worm liked best—the ones that nobody ever picked up to read.

Thus he became known as a bookworm. Not because he liked to read books (although he did enjoy reading a little now and then) but because he loved to nibble and chew and chomp on the pages.

The bookworm's favorite book to eat was the scriptures. The pages were nice and thin and easy to eat, and their taste was heavenly. He could always find a book of scriptures laying around the house unused.

Soon there were lots and lots of bookworms. They were in houses all over town, eating everyone's books—especially scriptures. The people were annoyed by these bookworms. They were tired of finding little holes in all the pages of their books, and they wanted to get rid of the little pests. They tried lots of different things, but nothing seemed to work.

One day, a young man was very tired of trying to get rid of the bookworms. He had just about given up hope of ever being rid of them. He decided to take a break. He sat down in a chair, picked up his set of scriptures, and began to read. Much to his surprise, he enjoyed reading very much. It gave him such a warm feeling inside. So good, in fact, that he decided to read from the scriptures every day and, as often as possible, read other good books.

As this young man read his scriptures every day, he noticed something wonderful happening—all the bookworms left. The man told all his friends, and they started reading too. Soon, everyone in town was reading and learning from all the good books. They all found that they were much happier too.

Everyone was happier except the bookworms that is. They had to go back to eating apples.

Who's getting the most out of your scriptures?

Have you picked them up lately?

INSTRUCTIONS

Make one copy of each picture on cardstock paper. Color as desired. Laminate and cut out the pictures. Glue a large craft stick on the back of each picture.

Door sign: Copy door sign on cardstock. Color as needed. Laminate. Cut along dark lines. Also cut along the dotted lines to create the hole for hanging on the doorknob.

QUIET !

Bookworm hard at work !

Bookmarks

Copy on cardstock. Color, cut, and laminate.

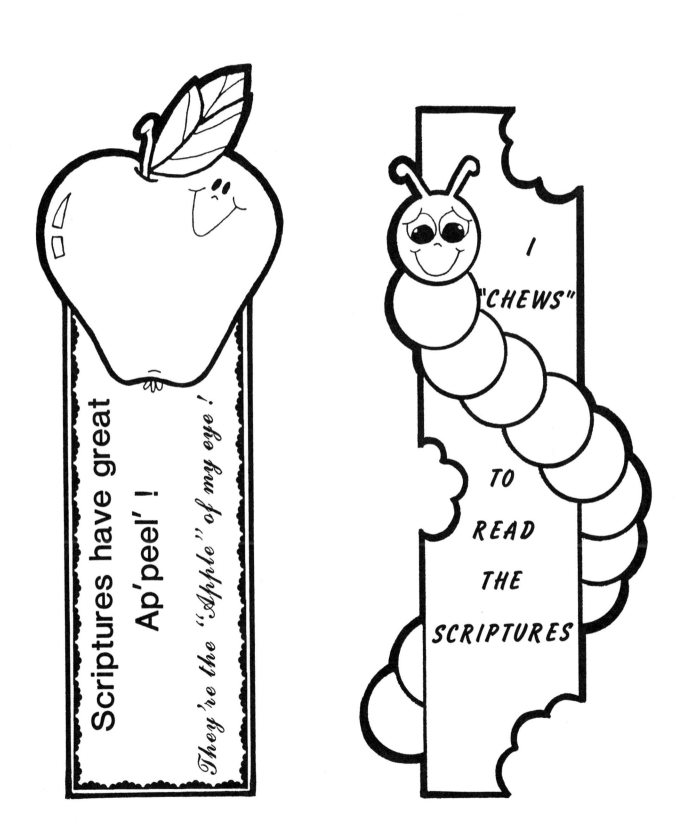

Scriptures have great Ap'peel'!

They've the "Apple" of my eye!

I "CHEWS" TO READ THE SCRIPTURES

Certificate

Copy on colored paper. Give to the children whenever a milestone has been reached.

Scripture Reading Award

Presented to _____ for "worming" his/her way inch by inch through the scriptures and for outstanding achievement in _____ .

Signed _____

Date _____

"worm'derful!"

Open Book

Can be used for badges, favorite scriptures, invitations, quotations, reminders, or any number of other things. Use your imagination. Its uses are endless.

Refrigerator Magnet

Copy on cardstock. Laminate and cut out. Hot glue a magnet on the back. Makes a cute handout.

Scriptures have great Ap'peel'!

Let's get to the 'Core' and read them today!

READING THE SCRIPTURES IS 'WORM' DERFUL

Badge

Copy on cardstock. Laminate and cut out. Add a small bow to the bottom to make it cute.

STEP BY STEP THROUGH THE SCRIPTURES...

INSTRUCTIONS

Cards: The questions for the game are from the four standard works. Each of the standard works has been given a different color. They are as follows: Doctrine and Covenants—yellow, Book of Mormon—blue, Pearl of Great Price—green, Bible—red.

Copy the shoe cards on the color of paper indicated at the bottom of each page. There is a blank page of shoe cards included so you can make up some questions.

Game Board: Color all the shoe prints, alternating the four colors of cards. Mount the two pages side by side on the inside of a file folder. Make sure the colors line up the same.

Spinner: Copy the spinner on cardstock. Color it using the four colors as indicated. Laminate everything. Cut out the shoe cards and spinner along dark lines. Put the spinner together with a brad. Now you're ready to play.

Game Rules: The first player spins the spinner. The player then advances to the first shoe space that is the same color as the spinner indicates. Another player then draws a card, again the same color, and reads it to the first player. If the first player can answer the question correctly, he is allowed to stay on that space. If he does not know the answer, he must go back to his previous space. All the players take turns spinning and answering questions. The first player to reach the open book of scriptures wins the game. The game may also be played with teams. Use the markers provided. When playing as individuals, you may wish to make or purchase more markers.

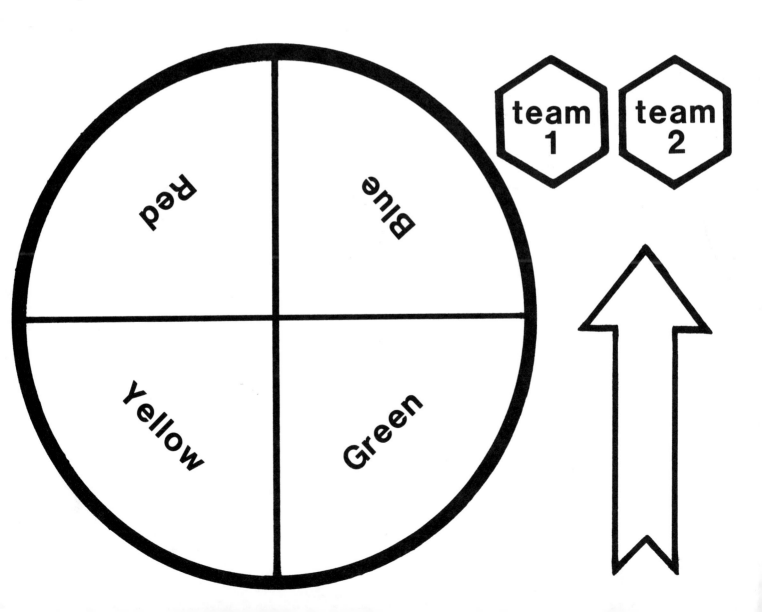

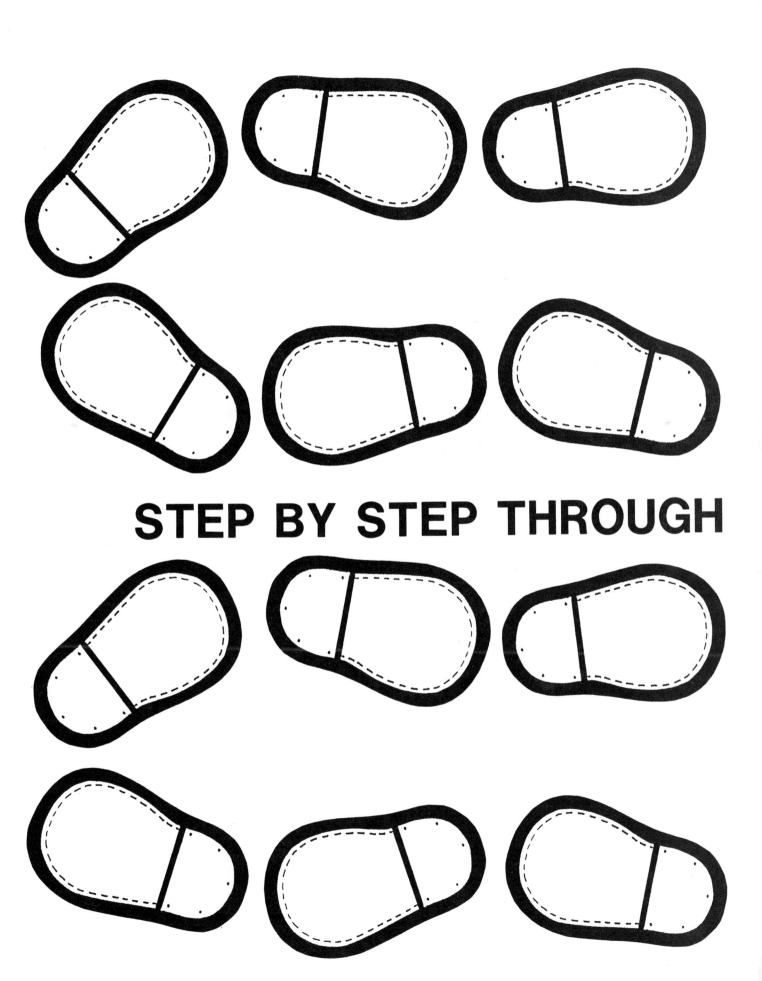

STEP BY STEP THROUGH

THE SCRIPTURES . . .

Finish

Start

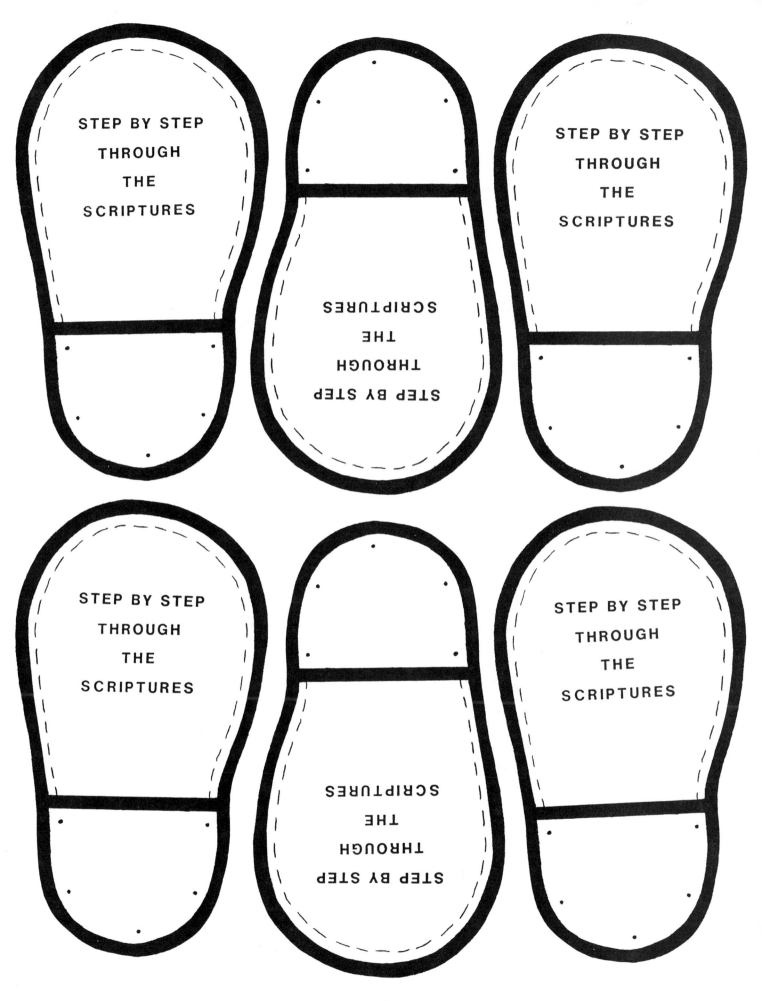

Copy on yellow paper.

What are the names of the two priesthoods?

Aaronic and Melchizedek

Who was also killed at Carthage Jail?

Hyrum Smith

What is the name of the man who was the first bishop of the Church?

Edward Partridge

Which section of the Doctrine and Covenants contains the sacrament and baptismal prayers?

Section 20

There are five things that the witnesses of the Book of Mormon saw. Name three of them.

The gold plates, sword of Laban, breastplate, Urim and Thummim, Liahona

What is the name of the jail where Joseph Smith was finally killed?

Carthage Jail

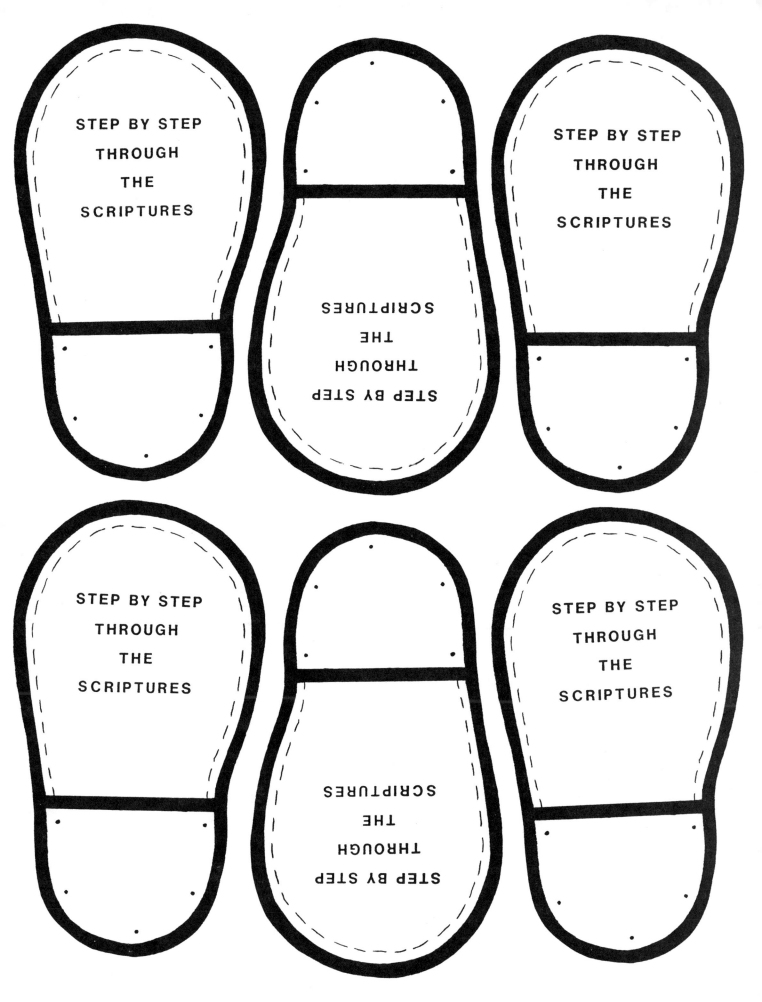

STEP BY STEP
THROUGH
THE
SCRIPTURES

Copy on yellow paper.

In what year was the Church organized?

1830

Name the town and state where the first temple was built in the latter days.

Kirtland, Ohio

Who appeared to Joseph Smith and told him about the golden plates?

The angel Moroni

Name the men who restored the Melchizedek Priesthood to the earth.

Peter, James and John

Which section of the Doctrine and Covenants talks about the Word of Wisdom?

Section 89

By what name was Adam known before coming to earth?

Michael

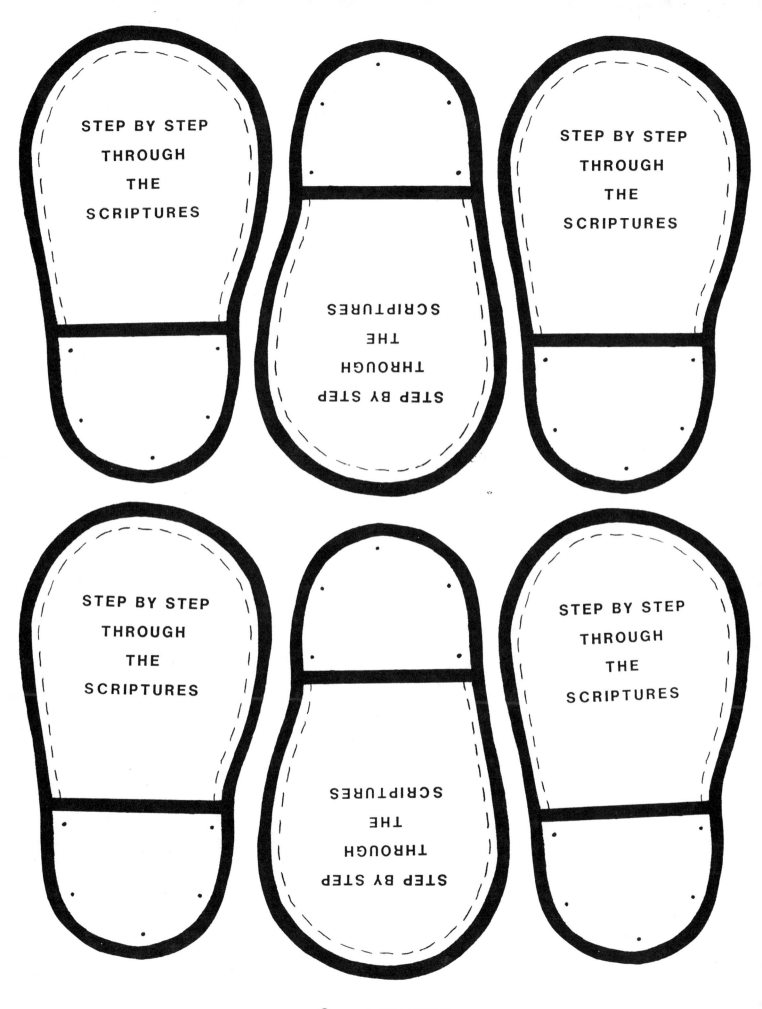

Copy on green paper.

Joseph Smith had the First Vision in what year?

1820

Who appeared to Joseph in the Sacred Grove?

God the Father and His Son

What is God's work and glory?

"To bring to pass the immortality and eternal life of man"

What is another name for the city of Enoch?

Zion

Who wrote the thirteen articles of faith?

Joseph Smith

One day on Kolob is equal to how many years on Earth?

1,000 years

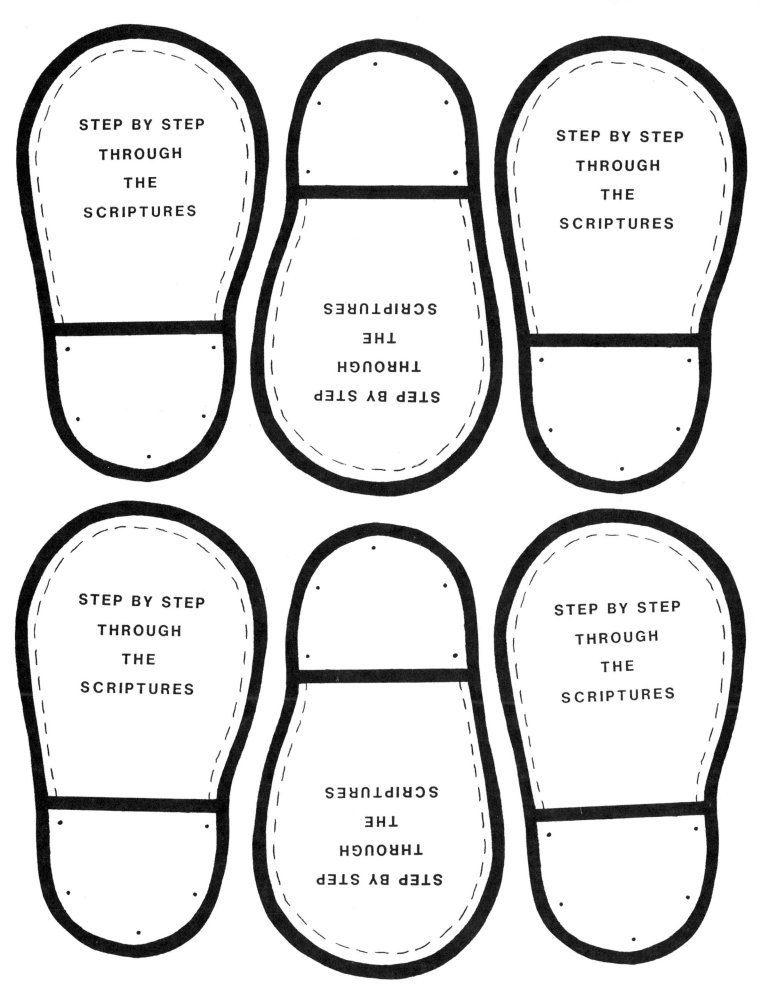

STEP BY STEP
THROUGH
THE
SCRIPTURES

STEP BY STEP
THROUGH
THE
SCRIPTURES

STEP BY STEP
THROUGH
THE
SCRIPTURES

STEP BY STEP
THROUGH
THE
SCRIPTURES

STEP BY STEP
THROUGH
THE
SCRIPTURES

STEP BY STEP
THROUGH
THE
SCRIPTURES

Copy on green paper.

Which article of faith talks about the organization of the Church?

Six

What was Joseph Smith's wife's name?

Emma Hale

What are the first principles and ordinances of the gospel?

Faith, repentance, baptism, and the laying on of hands

Who baptized Joseph Smith?

Oliver Cowdery

How many articles of faith are there?

Thirteen

Who was the first person on earth to be baptized?

Adam

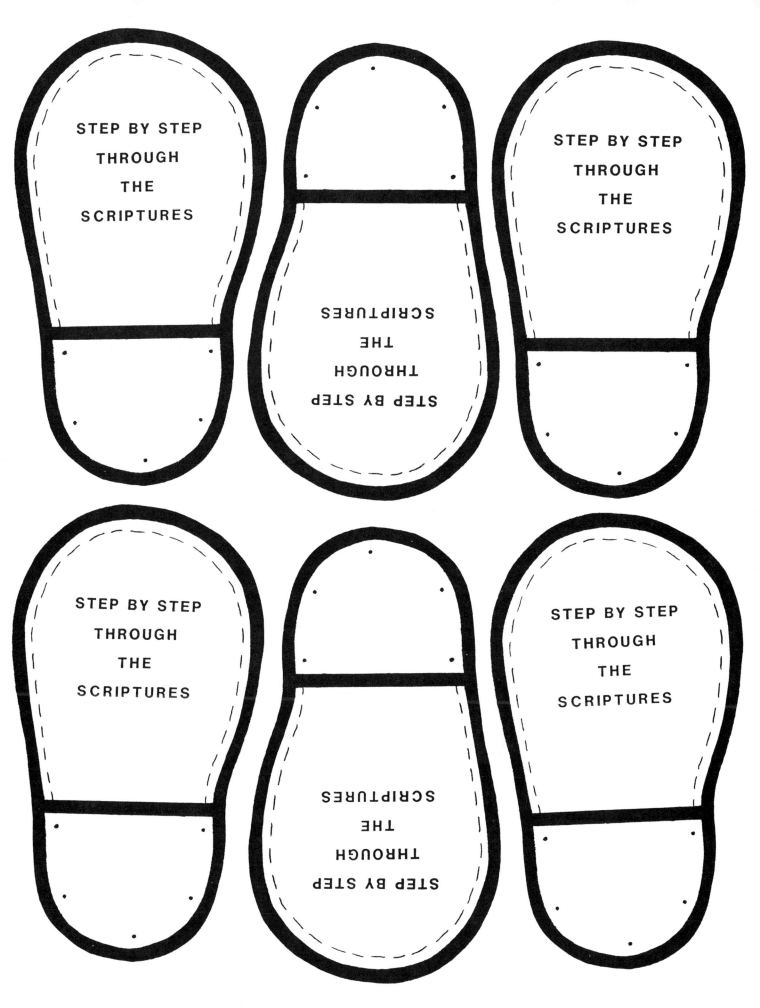

STEP BY STEP
THROUGH
THE
SCRIPTURES

STEP BY STEP
THROUGH
THE
SCRIPTURES

STEP BY STEP
THROUGH
THE
SCRIPTURES

STEP BY STEP
THROUGH
THE
SCRIPTURES

STEP BY STEP
THROUGH
THE
SCRIPTURES

STEP BY STEP
THROUGH
THE
SCRIPTURES

Copy on red paper.

Which of the sons of Jacob was sold into Egypt?

Joseph

Jesus was in the wilderness for 40 days and nights. What was he doing?

Fasting and communing with angels

Which four of Jesus' Apostles were fishermen?

Peter, James, John, Andrew

Esau sold his birthright to Jacob for what?

A mess of pottage

Samson killed 1,000 men with what weapon?

Jawbone of a donkey

How much did Judas receive for betraying Christ?

30 pieces of silver

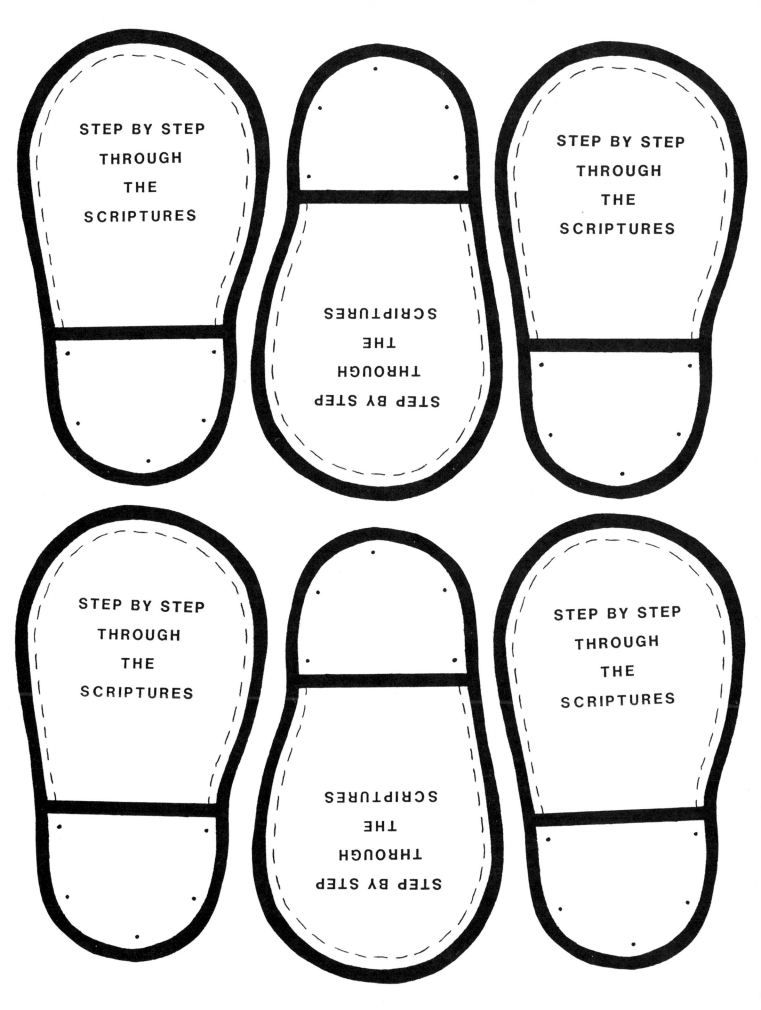

Copy on red paper.

Name the mountain where Moses received the Ten Commandments.

Sinai

Who baptized Jesus?

John the Baptist

Whose daughter did Jesus raise from the dead?

Jairus's

Name 6 of the 10 plagues.

Water turning to blood; frogs; lice; flies; sick animals; boils; hailstorms; locusts; darkness; death of all firstborn

What was Jesus' first miracle?

Turning water to wine

What did the Israelites eat while wandering through the desert?

Manna

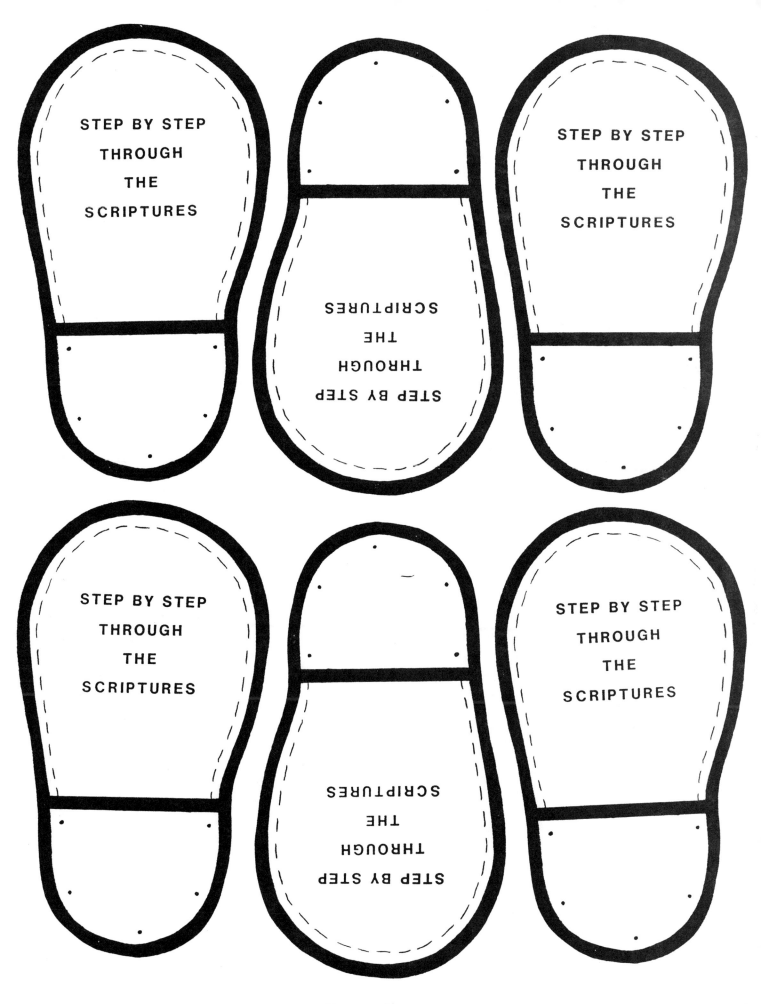

Copy on blue paper.

The Book of Mormon is another witness of whom?

Jesus Christ

The 2,000 stripling warriors said they were taught by whom to be courageous and valiant?

Their mothers

How long did Enos pray?

All day and all night

Alma the Younger and what men tried to destroy the Church?

Four sons of Mosiah

Why did Nephi and his brothers go back to Jerusalem?

To get the brass plates

Which Book of Mormon hero cut off some Lamanites' arms while protecting the king's flocks?

Ammon

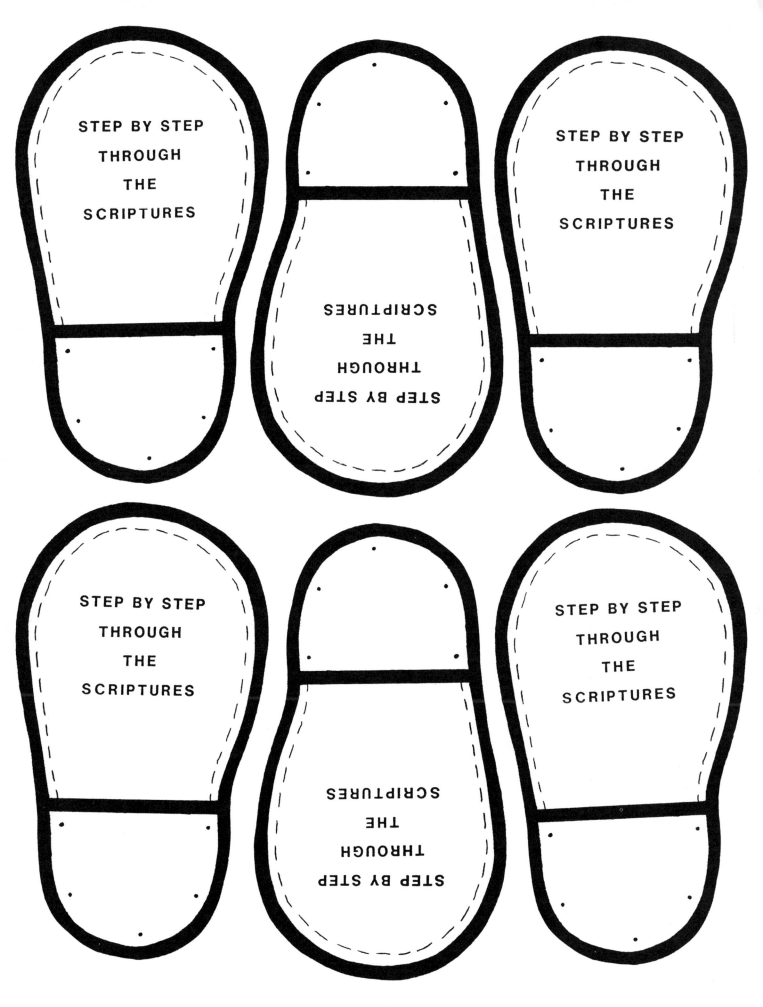

STEP BY STEP THROUGH THE SCRIPTURES

Copy on blue paper.

Who spoke from a large tower in his final address to his people?

King Benjamin

Which two sons of Lehi were rebellious?

Laman and Lemuel

Who buried the gold plates and later told Joseph Smith where to find them?

Moroni

What did the Jaredites use to light their barges?

Stones that were touched by the finger of the Lord

Who stood on a city wall and prophesied of our Savior's birth?

Samuel the Lamanite

What did the Lord give Lehi and his family that helped them find their way through the wilderness?

Liahona

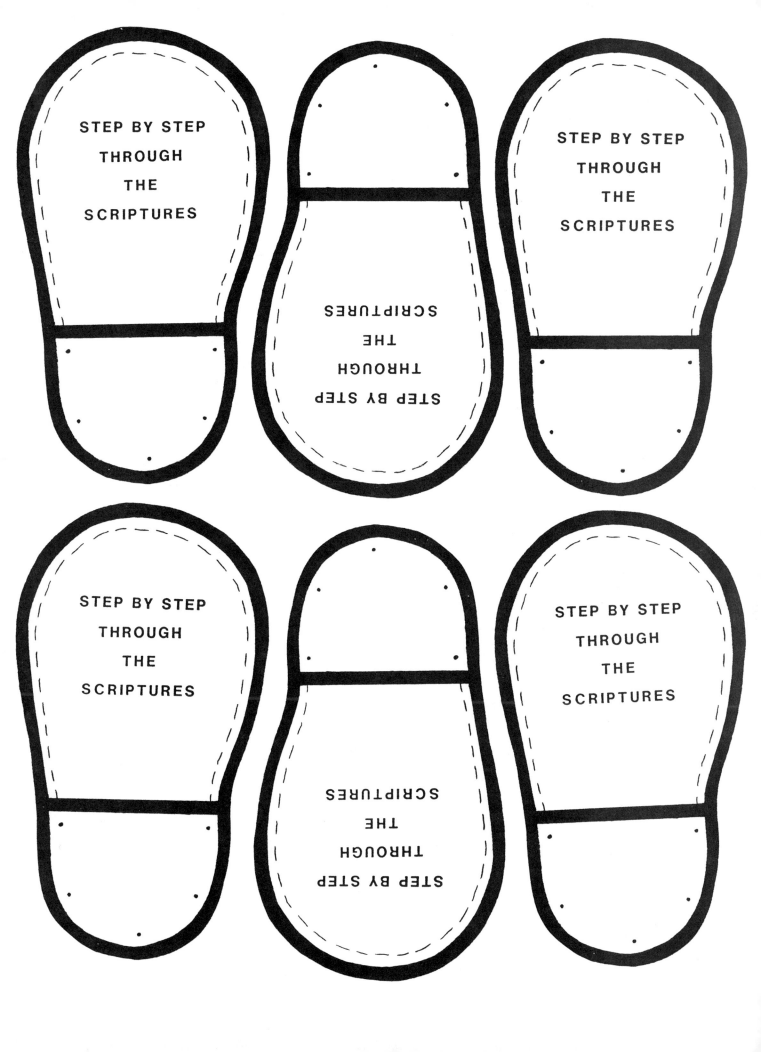

Answers

FEELINGS OF REVERENCE

Crossword answers:

- 1 Across: THOUGHTFUL
- 2 Across: HAPPINESS
- 3 Across: REVERENCE
- 4 Across: PEACEFUL
- 5 Across: SONGS
- 6 Across: GRATITUDE
- 4 Down: QUIT
- 6 Down: LOVE
- 2 Down: PRAYERFULL
- 1 Down: SCRIPTURES
- 3 Down: FEELING
- 5 Down: RESPECT

KEY WORD HIDE-A-WAY

A	D	M	O	N	I	T	I	O	N	A	D	W	G	J	K	T
B	R	D	A	B	H	M	O	P	G	K	C	E	C	L	K	E
H	I	A	T	O	N	E	M	E	N	T	F	C	D	A	A	N
L	H	J	C	L	S	X	R	S	S	A	C	B	Z	S	Q	
Q	N	O	W	C	M	F	W	M	A	H	L	L	X	U	V	T
S	V	R	X	F	L	T	X	C	E	A	B	A	N	Q	P	R
G	Z	G	R	I	A	E	D	B	I	M	O	I	W	K	N	I
I	Y	A	J	C	I	J	S	Q	K	C	N	M	N	H	K	B
F	V	N	F	M	D	C	S	S	G	O	D	H	E	A	D	S
T	O	I	K	E	J	C	D	I	O	Z	N	K	B	N	A	
S	R	Z	P	N	K	I	J	V	Y	F	K	A	C	D	C	F
P	S	A	Z	Z	V	N	J	K	I	K	S	B	A	S	J	I
Y	Q	T	R	A	N	S	L	A	T	E	V	F	X	T	Y	J
X	Y	I	Z	X	M	I	J	N	T	W	W	F	A	J	F	N
R	W	O	M	I	O	M	R	E	V	E	L	A	T	I	O	N
M	J	N	W	T	O	I	Y	X	O	F	M	O	U	B	T	U
F	I	R	S	T	O	P	R	I	N	C	I	P	L	E	S	H